UNDER THE BROOM TREE

Under the Broom Tree
© 2021 by Natalie Homer

Autumn House Press receives state arts funding support through a grant from the Pennsylvania Council on the Arts, a state agency funded by the Commonwealth of Pennsylvania, and the National Endowment for the Arts, a federal agency.

cover art: *White Wolf. Flora + Fauna 02* by Misha Ashton
book design: Tyler Crumrine

ISBN: 978-1-938769-99-3
Library of Congress Control Number: 2021939525

UNDER THE BROOM TREE

by Natalie Homer

AUTUMN HOUSE PRESS
Pittsburgh, PA

UNDER THE BROOM TREE

by Natalie Homer

AUTUMN
HOUSE PRESS

Pittsburgh, PA

Autumn House Press receives state arts funding support through a grant from the
Pennsylvania Council on the Arts, a state agency funded by the Commonwealth of
Pennsylvania, and the National Endowment for the Arts, a federal agency.

cover art: *White Wolf. Flora + Fauna 02* by Misha Ashton
book design: Tyler Crumrine

ISBN: 978-1-938769-99-3
Library of Congress Control Number: 2021939525

The first branch, father, that brushes
against your hat on the way home; that is
what I should like you to bring me.

– Brothers Grimm, "Cinderella"

CONTENTS

III.

INTERVIEW

I'm the right candidate because I know
      how some things stand in for others.
Cotton batting for snow. A small mirror for a frozen pond.
There is a light bulb inside the church
      that makes its plastic windows glow.

All I'm saying   is it must be nice
to arrange the world on a mantel,
then plug the lights in.

A mistake: passing the semi in the storm.

Nocturne sounds pretty, whatever it is.
An orange sky at night. My biggest weakness.

In ten years, I see myself pointing out a cardinal on a power line.

I'll tell you about the time I solved the problem
of what colors were meant by *oyster*, *tulip*, and *sidecar*.

Or when I cut hundreds of paper snowflakes
      to hang from the ceiling
            for someone else's honeymoon.

I can tell you a little more about myself.
Like snow in April, I am a tired sort of fearless.

A PLACE TO LIE DOWN

If I were a bee, I might build my home
in the gutted rind of a melon, or webbed between
the sun-bleached bones of a lion's rib cage.

Other professional experience:
noticing the weed flowering in the rain gutter
and doing nothing about it.

Eventually the water backs up,
bubbles the paint in the dining room.
It is not my paint,
    my rain,
        or my dining room.

Meanwhile, ants (ever practical) harvest cicada husks—
little funeral processions across the driveway,
and I read how butterflies

put themselves to bed in the late afternoon
which sounds so charming—
their wings like eyelet sheets.

What is home but a place to lie down? A place
to wake up in, as the bats in the church eaves do,
diving, unsynchronized, into the striated rainbow dusk.

DIORAMA OF ANXIETY ATTACK

In poems, dads are called *Father*
        and they carry guns and shut doors.
I had a dream about lambs and foxes
        and wanting to save them both,
walking in the line of fire
        then not being able to move.

Watching two people share a look
carves a jack-o'-lantern in my chest.

This week: another jealous thought removed, bandaged.

Something's always under construction.
At the zoo, the polar bear is "on vacation,"
the tunnel under her tank ruptured in blue light
but water can be a spectacle, too.

My eyeshadow is called caterpillar.
My blush: Red Queen.
A bird builds her nest outside the forestry building.
Within a week, it is removed.

Tell your secret   is the prompt I've been assigned.

The word *wallows* sounds to me like a love song
a bird might sing in the sad evening.

Don't worry   it is not the same bird
and this is not the same river
and you are not the same man.

WILD TONIC IN THE RAIN

The bee oracle on the ledge of my ear
doesn't know how to sing—only to dance.
I read her coded steps and she tells me
to slit open the envelope of an unmemorable dream
in which I clean someone's home,
try to find a place for her things.

Evening gathers into a pool. Lilac. What else?
On my fingers: bleach traces, and I remember
how long it's been since I lay awake
and heard the distant hush of the Pacific,
a memento to return to
during the ugly birth of spring.

For the season, anxieties hatch fresh.
I count out *if onlys* over and over into a well
that will never yield anything more than water,
though I remind myself—water is enough.
And those little jeweled insults? I drop them
on purpose. I have to fight back somehow.

DEAR ASTORIA

Have the skeleton ships succumbed
to barnacles and rust, the salt wash of the sea?

And the little A-frame named "It'll Do"—
is it still there, safe in the hemlock?

Mild-mannered Pacific,
I wanted so badly for you to be home.

Your palette, cool-toned: foam, moss, grotto.
The woodsmoke: sweet censer.

Easy to perch here at the edge of the world,
place of departure. Violet morning, starless dark,

where the water seems to *make* the glass,
not just smooth it.

Eight rings of the bell mean *end of watch*.
Rarely is suffering heard so clearly.

GOOD VIBRATIONS

Midsummer, webs stretch over the porch chairs, the peonies.
These small tenants of the world—*Cyclosa*—
dress in their own detritus:
corsets of exoskeleton and silk.
There's something comforting about camouflage—
seeing without being seen.

In the mail: a card from my grandmother.
It is unreadable, like the others have been,
the cursive hopelessly optimistic.

When she was young, she danced, won beauty pageants.
I guess you'd call her a prairie rose, my mom says.
I like to imagine her this way—bright again,
her face smoothed, a crown on her head—
misted, silver, the rhinestones like drops of dew.

Once, during a storm, lightning reached through the window,
hit the sewing machine. That's the story, anyway.
Her mother was sewing a wedding dress at the time.
The old joke: lightning aside, it's hard to work with lace.

Now she has wreathed herself, her home, her yard
in Goodwill finds, garage sale trinketry.
The house, built by her parents, has become an island
squeezed between a car lot, train tracks, a plumbing supply co.
In the backyard, between the walnut trees, a cracked fountain
waits, waterless—a ponytailed girl pouring air into dust.

TOPOGRAPHY PACIFIC

The yellow-tiled tunnel out of Portland is no portal,
no reason to hold one's breath, and it's easy to forget
how the smells seep into everything:
the acrid reek of a lumber mill, the dairy farms,
mildew feeding on mild rain, mild warmth.

> The magic is gone from this place,
> enchanted forest of my memory turned sodden, tepid.
> There is no one to blame for this   but me.

Everything has shrunk since the last time I was here:
the yard, the distance between landmarks, my grandmother
in her fleece pajamas, her skin grub-white and three sizes too large.
Seeing her naked is like seeing an unclothed child.
There is no reason to look away   but I do.

> Without snow, the Christmas decorations hang gaudy and sad.
> I keep staring at a white wooden sleigh, its sides the shape of swans.
> This home was my home, once, but hasn't been for years,
> and being here reminds me of all my fears,
> reminds me they were true; we were *white trash*, like people said.

The attic my sister and I explored as children is rotted now,
its steps no longer an adventure—just steps, dusty and narrow.
Even the apple tree has fallen on hard times.
Leaving, I note the Cadillac's window, cracked open,
leaves and rain and debris washed across the dash.

ATTIC OF THE SKULL

As children, we thought the old milk door was for fairies,
and on the willow's east side: a withered face in the bark.

> The garage was full of *treasure*, not junk,
> and we climbed the wobbling towers
> discovering a lamp with cola-colored glass,
> a huge stuffed monkey with a plastic face,
> one empty wing of a dollhouse.

Picking wild strawberries was a novelty then,
and still is, though they are tiny and tart.

> At some point, knowledge replaces faith
> and is called maturity.

Today: one emerald earring down the drain
and rain ripples the daffodils like wet paper.
Pulling weeds makes me remember our childhood dog
who tunneled to escape so often
that we finally stopped filling in the hole.

> If only memory was more like a library
> and less like an attic
> in which you must watch your step
> or fall through the floor.

AM I THE ONLY ONE HERE

after the sculpture by Arran Gregory, 2014

If the forest had a uvula, static, speechless
this would be it.

The self   reflected   of course.

Low hanging fruit made of chrome metal, steel wire.
Gentle mobile, raw diamond, you disco-shine.

Will each facet gather pollen?
A fine yellow film of dust?
Your cold face needs a cloth.

Beautiful manufactured loneliness:
                    Are you a beacon in a fairy tale?
                            The last pure thing to lead us home?

I HEAR YOU'RE DOING A GREAT JOB

The bridge from West Virginia to Ohio
is the mercury glass color of Oz,
but here the magic is melancholy,
corroded and coal-bled.

On the side of the road: twin fawns,
white spots like wildflowers on their flanks.
I never pray, but I ask God to keep them safe,
to find their mother   to lead them home.

The gray-green membrane between spring and summer
is my event horizon   and I envy all things
from the Corona Borealis to the rat's accordion rib cage,
flexible as wings.

I'd like to transpose myself with the ironweed,
to assume its tall, graceful stem,
its slender lean,
its violet diadem—
and it can have me.

SUBURBAN ORCHESTRAL

Tulips, glass rabbits, and little moons,
scratched and shivered, their braille messages
unreadable constellations under my fingertips.
Refrigerator cold exhaled against the dish,
dropped dyes swimming smokelike in a vinegar pool.

Sanity walks a tightrope.
Snow-crunch of exam table paper, and the needle
slips into my hand, suave as a dance partner.
Daffodils know to hold back
for the opportune moment.

I want to be *believed*—
and this year, I won't mistake
the iris leaves for weeds.
I will right the toppled bricks
the rain-soaked soil has heaved.

DORMANCIES

Emptiness, absent for a while, claws out of its hole.
Friends die back to the ground as the heat of summer arrives.

He was still alive in this book, she said,
then heard her own words.

The bleeding heart hangs its ornaments
and I solicit the cherry blossoms for a private conversation.

In the dream, my teeth casually come loose. I tongue the gaps.
The meaning is the one you'd expect.

An important question: what bird would you be?
I said swan.   You said you didn't care for birds.

On a dewy summer morning, I walk through a spiderweb
on accident. Like so much else, it clings and follows.

FEAR OF LOSS AT ANY MOMENT

The iris spends itself in one afternoon.
Ivy and mosquito bubble my skin
with their common poisons
                                        and I wonder
when this fragile happiness
I've spun for myself   will collapse.

Stay close I urge the young rabbit
as he nears the road.
Is he the same one on the lawn
each abalone evening?

Last night, in the dream, it felt so good
to be held. I succumbed immediately.

LIQUOR OUTLET

It starts in the citrus hour of evening,
my mind on an imagined meridian
where I can smell the sting through the sugar.

Behind the storefront window,
an arched tentacle, black,
but purple in the Clarendon filter of memory.

Driving past becomes a ritual,
and the displays shift with the seasons.

Now, a neutron star
in the form of a disco ball,
its flashes silver drops
of rain, a verse illustrated in real time.

I imagine what's next:

a paper parasol stamped with cherry blossoms,
or a Ferris wheel with frosted bottles in each gondola.

Going up is easier than coming down,

and the top notes never last long
because they are the sweetest.

THE BRAVERY OF COTTON

sheets in a thunderstorm
clipped to the line,   forgotten.

And later, tumbling around the hot dark,
static stars wheeling from the fibers.

Sometimes I picture it raw,   still on the stem,
plucked and pressed to a bleeding cheek,
seeds and all.
As if healing were so simple.

The fields quiver with boll weevils
whose tiny teeth tear their own insulation,
feeding   like children in a fairy tale
on their one chance for shelter,
seeing it disappear—melt—
from soft flossy whirls of white into sugary grit.

Someone told me cotton scents are completely artificial,
that real cotton smells like sweat, or like something burning.

And now I see that the fields are on fire,
that maybe they were always on fire,
and I've been standing here, at the edge of an oily ocean   burning.

CORALBONE BLOOM

after necklace sculptures by Mariko Kusumoto

You, perfect   but blank.
A dress form, beige, standard.

Until you erupt. Springtime underwater.
Gauze tendrils, growth in radial symmetry.

Paper lanterns inflate on your décolletage,
gentle as mushrooms after rain.

Though you are not lit up, you feel buoyant,
worthy of silk and chiffon. Worthy of your seat
on the train, your place in the universe.

Everyone will want to reach out and touch you
but you are too fragile to be that kind of girl.

PLEASANT GHOSTS

Wild tiger lilies swath the roadsides.
I look for the flash-and-die green light
of fireflies: electric diamond dust in the dark trees.

This night: another dream in which I discover
hidden rooms within hidden rooms
and those forgotten objects from childhood:
a cloth doll, tin pail, jar of found feathers.

This house retains its pleasant ghosts—
in the spare bedroom, skeletal leaves
pressed under the pale pistachio paint,
and in a basement storage closet:
penciled notes on the wall.

What is it in us that seeks skin for skin's sake?
At any rate, the morning was an invitation
and I answered it.

TORPOR

When I hear the mud wasps buzz and boil through the wall
I knock, and to their credit, they stop, like chastised neighbors.

Their tunnels, pasted to the brick, are called pipe organs,
but the music they make is anxious,
each voice masculine, the violence implicit.

I have never been good at taking care of these things—
problems that have multiplied and made nests.

Hazy July ends in rain,
and the trees lose their tender branches to the storm.
I am always the one who stays behind,
who clings to home.

Against the rain-dipped sky, dyed pale, a Yale blue envelope,
the silhouette of a single bat replaces the birds,
a slower, more humble creature—
one who knows the value of silence.

INTERIOR ARCHITECTURE

Carved into a birch: the initials BKO,
and a Buffalo nickel hidden in the knot.
How pleasing to come across another's secrets.

Water striders skate the edges of the lake
in which a church is submerged
except for the steeple, which rises—glacial.

I kept it for a long time,
that quartz with the ghost of another crystal
blooming in its glassy depths,

thinking it meant something,
the way a female fetus carries all the eggs
she'll ever have—an hourglass within her

before she even knows of existence. Outside,
dry lightning. Azalea reaches toward the window,
begging to be let inside.

MY MOTHER SENT CARDS

I didn't respond to.
I thought of her
sitting on a porch by herself,
   or crouching low to take pictures of wildflowers
      with a disposable camera.

I knew her handwriting   the way you know a pet has been hit by a car.

The drive back home always took two days,
and I threw up with the stress of it
in a motel bathroom haunted by old smoke and cheap soap.
Disposable razors. Cold cream. Diet Coke.

Whenever she reached out to touch my hair   I moved away.

As desert relaxed into evergreens
my sister and I looked forward to the exact bend
where the river ran through a rusted truck's passenger window
and out the driver's side.

         I want to think of her as strong.
         As someone who doesn't need me.

We asked her   *Why doesn't someone move it?*
                     Why doesn't someone take it away?

A HIDING PLACE, A SURPRISE

One always begins to forgive a place as soon as it's left behind.
—*Charles Dickens*

The town was one part nuclear accident, one part prayer.
I haven't forgiven it.

I want to say *hate* but that's not what I mean.
I mean the feeling of seeing another treeless neighborhood
being sowed, fire hydrants first, where a pasture had been,
or August baptisms in the Snake River,
the believers coming up soaked and squinting like newborns.

I drove the same circuit of country road in the washed-out evenings.
The landmarks: a willow near the canal bridge,
a hobbit-style house set into a grassy hill,
irrigation sprinklers in a barley field.

Everything in me ached
for a different place, a different life.

Now, I think of this ceramic cowboy boot,
how the russet top lifted off to reveal
a hiding place   my mother said, for jewelry or coins,
but right where the ball of the foot would be
was a black beetle, built-in, painted.
The first time I opened it she said   *Surprise.*

Going home always felt like defeat—
the turbines in a ragged line, twirling their white batons
on the hills that looked like a dusty velvet painting.
They don't look real   my mom would insist.
You could lick your finger and smudge them away.

SUNFLOWERS IN THE MEDIAN

Everything is a union of one kind or another.
Foothills know this. Highways too.

In the median—wild sunflowers for miles.
Cheerful, unassuming. They are no one's bouquet.

My dad and I try very hard to seem at ease
with each other. We comment on the bison

stampeding across the casino's electric sign.
Pixilated, their clouded breath leads them

again and again over an imagined prairie.
Later I will make this drive every day,

memorize little landmarks: the row of cottonwoods,
the peaked shelter at the reservoir's edge,

the water towers marking the reservation.
I will become so sick of the sagebrush,

the snow and the sun, an incessant blue sky,
that I'll wilt to think of this place being home.

But today it's a morning I'm not sorry to be awake for,
so that's something. And no one mourns a coyote

with his russet head resting on the road's shoulder.
Neither does the ditch fire elicit sympathy.

The sunflowers did not teach me this,
but their small faces look so cheerful

bouncing in the slipstream of traffic—
I will believe anything they say.

DIVINATION

Flies are in love with silence
     the way a coyote loves a highway.
They resurrect in the windowsill,
the October sunlight a mouth of white
teeth.   All bark and no bite.

A dowsing rod leads me to an open grave.
The dogs roll in the carcass,
shaved of skin   overgrown with sage.

The veins have become vines,
no longer velvet, no longer shining.
Hooves harden to stone
and roll   downhill.

The entrails keep quiet.

On the walk home
I look for Equuleus   a little horse
         a little scar
in the sky
   but cannot find it.

DUST ON HORSES

On the tack room mirror. Something to run a finger through,
something to shine in the ocher light, motes like tiny suspended jellyfish. Something
to settle on a spectrum of dirty neon wraps, on the pinned ribbons, curdled white.
Something to choke on, in the heat, while the sun cuts and runs,
leaves me pressed like a bluebell, between Lamentations and Ezekiel,
to wither and dry. Alternately,   the light   in gradient   labeled like a paint chip:
Daisy Chains   Butterscotch Silk   Honeysuckle Bareback Queens   Golden Braids
Sweat. The opposite of dust. A clean, tingling smell, alfalfa rain.
A shining undulation that swells and melds across legs, rumps, sides.
Pharaoh was not *mine*, you said, and were right.
I snapped a carrot in half, pretended it was your neck.
Such is the unabashed violence of childhood.
Yesterday someone told me   *Your instincts are more important than praise*
and last night I dreamed of a hoof pick, and a black leg,
the hollow heart scraped clean,   how the body balances   how it sways.

GLUE MARKET

and how raw the sunlight was

at hoof harvest

chipped crescent moons

the dogs carry away to gnaw

so what do you care

your pinned blue ribbon mare

all swivel ears and velvet veins

invisible lunge lines

sky full of spurs

fluted, marrow-sucked bones

its loamy shoveled holes

how do you like the summer now

covered in webbed afterbirth

dirty mirror, rotten apple

canter canto contrapasso

evening comes on like a stiff lasso

broken legs

red rover red rover send Pharaoh right over

MORNING GLORY POOL

In Yellowstone, Morning Glory trumpets from the earth
a prismatic funnel web / a cornucopia
its fragile scalloped edges goldenrod and rust.

Tourists used to take spoons and pry the crust for souvenirs,
            or else throw things in. Everything is take or give.
Some things you'd never understand,
                                    like boots / bottles / a sofa.
Other things you would:
                        delicate handkerchiefs from another era,
like a *bon voyage* from a retreating ship,
and coins / little copper wishes meant to dissolve.

They didn't know bacteria are delicate and prone to fits,
mottling like mood rings, the water taking on their altered pigments,
cooling as the cultures sprawl.

Conveniently, geysers can be artificially induced / like a womb / to erupt,
and Morning Glory has birthed horseshoes / towels / a drone.
But its original blue is a torn dress, long gone.

The metaphors abound
                    but for now
the sulfur is churning my stomach.
I retreat on the creaking boardwalk that needs to be replaced,
crippling into the caustic water with each passing year.

IN MY DESERT

We wash our feet in dust & hear our long-
dead hounds bay underground. We've always lived
this way. Our hair frays like sagebrush. When
the sky purples with storm, our hearts beat
a little faster. Wind rings the bells. The river
is lost. *Spring up, O well.* Slow and steady
splits the canyon. No more altar calls, please.
Every barn's a wedding, every red-throated
bird a prophecy. Less thunder in the
mouth means we shouldn't sing. Antlers drop
their hollow bone, our mothers twist their wedding rings.
The pastor asks us to stand. The corona
swings. A chapel is a dry creek bed &
baptism means drowning secondhand.

OVERLOOK

The valley sheds its hazy shawl at night,
becomes an electric incantation.
Inside, moths flicker in the stairwell light—
pale, dust-soft. The horse kicks her water trough
and underground, the bones of long-dead dogs
whittle thinner every year. Aspens quake
their silver fans, wind rings the tone-deaf chimes
and the hollow in my chest collapses,
a little. I'm tired and getting older
in this desert that did feel like home, once.
In spring, the sagebrush will powder its hair
saffron, and maybe things won't seem so bleak
when the fields blush green for a week or two,
and thunder rips the placid sky in sheets.

EVERY SEVEN YEARS

The things you never want to see again keep replaying.
For me—pink baby mice in the entry of an Albertson's
and the man in front of me   his boot   no second thoughts.
His wife looked back at me   and I looked away.
I am good at looking away.

The town was called Swan Lake
but there were no swans   and there was no lake.
We split the barbed wire, then climbed through.
Later, I washed my hands in a gas station bathroom,
the liquid soap scented a bright, artificial grape.

Every seven years, a new body completely.
A myth, but a nice one.
Nice to imagine.   Strangers can be kinder than friends,
you know.   Like the men who pushed my car out of a ditch.
I opened my door to say thank you
but they didn't hear me   over the wind and the snow.

IMMERSION

Crumpled swan   waterlogged   origami
one wing in a frayed salute   to the wind,

its neck coiled like a fine silver chain.
Across the water the carousel played

a clumsy, bright organ song. Now, the scrape
of the park worker's net over the fence

struggling to heft the body up, and me
watching, for free, the unintended show.

*

Swans are baptized daily—no seafoam green tub on a church stage,
no drowned spider like a tiny black rib cage on the surface

of the water. No carnations after.   But I am no swan.
Was no swan   when I stood near the fire's hot breath in the dark,

in stiff, seafoam green underwear   looking to the cabin's loft,
the only light in our small wilderness.

It was so cold. And we were so tired. And I wanted to hear
that satisfying clink of the pull-chain, closing the light out

as folded wings do.

*

Water can speed up decomposition.
This much we know. Peeling skin like petals—

white, of course. But I've never been baptized
and I fell asleep on my wedding night

and woke up to the golden October
wake the tourists left when they went away

and the flies clotted in the window sizzling
to life, graceless lunging. The light, distilled.

GENEALOGY

The fish is graceful in his element
but in my hand becomes slick muscle,
becomes the grip of breathlessness.

When scaling, avoid pressing too hard.
This is good advice in general.

The guts just go in the water? I ask.
My father replies   *What else would you do with them?*

*

Cleaving is the secret meaning of life, if you want to know.

A dim, warm science classroom surfaces in memory—
and I wonder: do we classify death
as a physical or chemical change?
The frog is a centerfold.
We spill her eggs.

*

I'd like to be barren the way Craters of the Moon is,
with its lava tubes, its sagebrush
like a flower behind the ear.

I'm having trouble finding the heart, I write.
What I mean is   the crux.
They are not the same thing.

*

Remember: water is generous and will carry anything away.
We should all be so lucky.

EQUITY

One source suggests Idaho's name can be attributed to a mining lobbyist who claimed it came from a Shoshone word meaning, "Behold! the sun coming down the mountain."

A pheasant flees into the roadside field,
and the foothills are capped in flames—
each day a brew of sun and haze,
the quiet violence of rural life.

Off the highway, little landmarks draw my attention:
grain elevator among the sagebrush,
abandoned mill covered in Mormon graffiti:
ELDER PERRY WELCOME HOME / I LOVE YOU SHAYLEE P.

That every new house replacing sweet barley fields
can be occupied   is a puzzle to me.
The usual lures, I suppose.
Safe.   Cheap.   Open space.

Homesickness for these dry valleys
is a white butterfly I tweeze easily from my abdomen.

*

Meanwhile, eighty miles north, my favorite mountain
on the eastern edge of the Centennials
retains its old nickname: Rain-in-the-Face,
a Lakota chief, a chiseled visage looking skyward.

It is harder to forget this place,
strung like a rubber band, taut, somewhere inside me.
Sometimes I understand the desire to possess the land,
to hoard what is best for oneself.

If I could, I would draw the mountain to me,
rope off the river's outlet, the field of wild mint.
I'd put a fence up around each swath of Indian paintbrush,
the old railroad bridges, the log lodges, out-of-date.

I'd retreat into that selfish pleasure of owning,
for certain, what can belong to no one.

TELEMETRY

Centennial is the perfect name for the mountains—
a silver word, like the silver radar dome on the peak,
little sentinel. The vintage Books of Mormon on the cabin's shelf
have seen no white winters, shuttered in the dark as they are—
only heard the snow settle on the roof,
the soft crush of footfalls outside.
It is safer, of course, to keep myself at a distance.
I learned this the hard way. The coyotes, too.

SEARCH PARTY (1.)

snowpack to the roof   icicles to the ground
          the power lines are down
in the crisp   silver
                    mirror
                         of winter
my cries touch the peaks
                              return
                    to chime
                         the delicate bones of my inner ear—
their forgettable shapes
                    seahorse?
                    shovel?
                    teacup?
moun•tain (n.) synonym // a rough-cut jewel
                                        priorities shift
                                        when you're alone
you can scream to the woods
everything you ever wanted to say
                              I dreamed
          a literal wolf at the door   and a lighter in my hand
     what intrusion worries me so?   and what violence
                              would I be willing to use
                              to keep it at bay?

the morning   has gold in its mouth, we can agree—
but what about the afternoon? the evening?
                                        grief goes stale
                                        in the back of the cupboard
                                        to be found next season
and emptied
                    wilderness: a thing to be rescued from
the past—even more so
                              stay where you are
                              is the usual advice,
if you find yourself having wandered

SEARCH PARTY (II.)

Still lost   and sending up flares
in the lullaby blue dusk of snow and stars.

Just speak your mind   is good advice
but I've ignored more pressing things before.

Woodpile. Haystack. Forest. No place
to play house. Exodus means rescue

yourself. Another tip: follow the river.
You wanted me gone, so I left

but I still have my tin can, string stretched
all the way back to Idaho, listening

to static, to birds and squirrels perched on the line,
to clothespins and people playing limbo.

I suppose we could all use a map,
a red dot that says YOU ARE HERE.

If you ever picked up the other can
I would say   *Come find me.*
I would say   *What took you so long?*

SUMMIT

I wish the wild mint would bake its scent into my skin,
and I could drag it behind me, a train of silvery lace.

It never does, and that's okay.
It is enough to smell it now.

It's grizzly season, my father says.
The outlet burbles, unconcerned.

I say a small prayer of thanks that the sun is veiled,
that it is replaced by an indigo bruise,
heavy with electricity
and cool rain.

The cars' rushed spray on the distant highway
is a seashell to my ear. The sound isn't blood. It's ocean.

The mountain is called Chief.
The mountain is called Rain-in-the-Face.

We drive up, stand on the forehead
after the ATVs have growled away
and look vaguely in the direction of Henry's Lake.

As we're leaving, he notices a clump of blue.
Forget-me-nots, I say, incorrectly.

He says,   I would have never known.

UNDER THE BROOM TREE

1 Kings 19:4–8

Sister, do you remember those cloth dolls,
goldenrod and cornflower, yarn hair, happy freckles?
The ones we found in the cupboard under the stairs?
We were friends, then, and I followed you
outside, carrying plastic dishes, a wooden high chair,
painted storybook bears fading from the backrest.

We called the lodgepole pine a broom tree
for its brushy branches that we broke off
and used to sweep the dirt in our little estate,
our playhouse in the Idaho mountains.

A smooth stone, baked in the sun, became a golden loaf,
we spooned sap as honey,
and sagebrush in water made the accompanying soup.

We were not weary then,
and we knew nothing of Elijah
and little of God for that matter.
Our coals and stones, bread and water
were our own, and surely no miracle.

Wildflowers put on their usual pageant.
We pressed Indian paintbrush to our cheeks and lips,
believing the petals' pigment would transfer.
You have always glowed golden and peach
and I was jealous of you even then—
of your long blonde braids and your slender hands.

Much had changed by the time, years later, I sat alone
in my windowless basement bedroom, the carpet ripped out,
the whole house made skeletal and echoing.
Outside, the wind sang its strange, sad howl
and swept snow across the road in milky tendrils.
I prayed for a convenient death
while you were upstairs, laughing your golden bell laugh.

I miss you, sister—
who you used to be, who I used to be
when we wove ourselves together without thought
so few years ago.

DEAR IDAHO—

I remember how your canals went dry at the end of summer. And how those round hay bales, dropped in perfect intervals, cast their pointed shadows. Here there is no hay. Instead, I learn the names of things: *Spicebush swallowtail* for the large black butterflies dusted with cobalt and rust, *Hackberry emperor* for the little brown ones with so many false eyes. No, I can't come back. Please don't ask again. Last time you wanted to know some things that stood out to me. Here they are: 1. an infinity symbol, freshly black, on the cashier's arm. 2. the silver glint of a plane and its twin jet streams in the too-blue sky. Last night, the fire spat at me and I scooted back, reminded of how I used to plan escapes. What I would take, what I would leave. You have to understand: going home means being in the place I was when I wanted to die.

ORGANIC GEOMETRY

The frosted, early morning moon
wears its pocked pregnancy at that unflattering stage
three-quarters full, that I don't know the name of.

My friend would know.
When she cried off and on throughout the night
I tried to look as distraught as possible.

Back at home, I stand outside the door,
watching an orb weaver in her silk—
torn dress mended one dutiful thread at a time.

VETERANS DAY

The hills in autumn: a patchwork quilt. Familiar thought, but comforting, still.
And the hunter behind the church—sometimes opportunity is unwelcome.
What happened to the flint of obsidian I kept for years? I want it back
suddenly, and without reason. The gunshots come in groups of six
on silver Saturday mornings, a mile off. Firing range, stocked pond.
Each wispy egg sac I see, I crush. It will keep us safe, if I do this enough.

RETURN TO SENDER

My doe with the limp is one fawn short since spring.
Sometime later, in the low moan of a snowstorm
she canters back to the woods, alone.

Yearly pilgrimage to Ohio—past factories and sallow fields,
to the tired town where a smell like cherry tobacco
settles over everything, a fine dusting of snow.

We sleep in the house of lives already lived,
dust in the corners, carpets worn thin,
and listen to the grandfather clock clear its melodic throat.

I could never live here, I say, and mean it.
But going home, we drive through a neighborhood I love
and I change my mind for a moment—

seeing these storybook houses—their scrollwork, lace edges,
where the paint is always fresh and each window holds a light
framed by lace curtains. I wonder who lives here—

who places a white dollhouse in an upstairs window,
who sweeps the walks so carefully, who scents the air
with sweet woodsmoke—what clean, well-crafted lives?

ANOTHER SMALL FAILURE

In this season of scarcity, compassion also wanes.
Silver is nice, for a while.

The boy on my porch mutters an apology.
He doesn't really mean it, and I don't really forgive him.

A weather-faded ribbon twirls up a bare branch of the crab apple,
and dead leaves knit together in the gap of the sliding doors.

In your church, I am an outsider, a visitor
who doesn't know the hymns or repetitions,

who is not allowed to take the Eucharist
and who shies, as unbroken horses do, from hands on my forehead.

WHAT YOU'RE REALLY LOOKING FOR

Ants announce spring from the corners of the house,
their neat swarms quiet and inevitable.

The bleeding heart is back, no thanks to me.
Its blossoms bend their vine:
a collarbone's grace.
With each day, the pink fades.

Despite everything, we are not yet saved.

I am disappointed when I realize
the tapping on the window isn't rain   but moths.

To pass the time, I browse engagement rings—an endless scroll.
It helps to want something obtainable.

This is me   on my knees   in a parking lot
trying to lure a stray cat out from under a car
and a girl from the bar saying   *Leave it.*
You aren't doing it any favors.

MEMORIAL DAY

The bleeding hearts have husked into pink paper. They crumble
when I'm not looking. This town empties in summer.

Meanwhile, reservoirs refill, insects plan their revival,
and I realize you can miss a thing before it's gone.

I knew I would miss the Bannock Range
as it filled my windshield every day,

the way the mountains darkened to tanzanite—
the snow immaculate on the peaks.

My family was a different story.

I put two petal-colored envelopes in the mailbox,
one for each mother. Both were indifferent

when I told them that the deer are everywhere here,
on the side of the road, yes, but also alive

on the lawn at dusk, velvety and mirror-still.
Yesterday, I dropped Skittles into blue champagne,

photographed the string of mushrooms in the yard,
listened to the highway, the rain.

APERTURE

A couple screams at each other in the still afternoon.
I decide Queen Anne's lace is my kind of flower.

> An impossible series of birds flocks to the trellis,
> disappearing one at a time into the grape leaves.
> When I pull back the vines,
> I expect to see a gown made of plumage,
> each hollow little bird hovering
> to form its share of hem or sleeve.

The breeze brings a whiff of garbage, but it is not unpleasant.
The neighborhood pretends not to hear the woman, left behind,
crying after being called a fat whore.

> Webs stretch from surface to surface all over the porch.
> They are made of sunlight.
> If only they were sturdier
> they could be bridal veils
> curtain sheers
> or doilies under cakes.

The three stepping stones in the yard
I found last year
have sunk again into the grass,
and this time I don't feel like unearthing them.
The last residents left them
along with toys around the yard—
a rubber shark, a Spider-Man figurine,
a bouncy ball, clouded colors like a jawbreaker,
half buried under the bleeding heart.

> Sometimes I feel like a witch, sometimes a kept woman.
> I drag the garbage to the dumpster, use my hand to tear
> the webs, retrieve a foam ball from under the hemlock tree.
> Eventually the crying quiets, as it generally does,
> without me having to do anything.

FOURTH OF JULY

Some nights, I ride my bike around the church parking lot
while frogs bellow from the nearby woods,
and I note the rabbits' absence this year.

The neighbors stake tiny flags along their driveway.
I glue the Bible's spine, underline a psalm in colored pencil.

At the nursery I visit my friend,
look for something with a romantic name—
Icelandic Poppy.   Champagne Bubbles.
I plant it on the north side of the house
and it looks lonely in its single clump,
the flower blooming in solitude,
a tiny smear of orange and yellow.

I had a dream about my teeth again.
The internet interprets:
a compromise that is costly to you.

I squeeze the brakes   then coast.
My lungs are cabbage moths. My tongue, a stone.

HOROSCOPE

I ask for a sign   and God sends balloons
a stray clump of white and blue
from a baby shower, maybe,
shrinking into the sky more and more every second.

Thunder cracks the summer wide open.

I heft the vacuum downstairs to the basement
to remove the creeping gray lives flourishing in corners.
So thin, I think.   I judge bodies even as small as these

and it's weird how reading a name can hurt so much.

Yes, *kintsugi* is a nice way to mend a broken bowl with gold,
but you can't deny a new one is cheaper and easier,
if you can do without the glimmer.

SOUVENIR

My husband calls, but the wind cuts him off.
I rinse maggots from the trash can to pass the time,
wanting to be where he is, in a humid tourmaline evening.
Before we disconnect, I hear my name
spoken across a continent, an ocean.

*

Shame, that tired perennial,
reminds me the skull is no treasure cave.
This season's offering: a memory. Me at thirteen,
staining the corral in the impossible sun.
Even after dark, no one called me in.

I stumbled blindly, painting the shed's last spidery corner,
then snuck in through the back door,
peeled off my dusty clothes in the bathroom,
and heard my name—the way you never want to hear your name—
through the vents from upstairs.

*

Like a seashell, I kept my maiden name,
little souvenir—brittle trophy.
Today I came across a meaning of it online:
a pool in a hollow—
unexpected. Sort of beautiful. Probably untrue.

GRAVEDIGGING, 5:00 AM

I catch my breath in the humid dark,
the rain   unsure of itself
and the insects, anonymous,
pinching vaguely at my arms.

As periwinkle folds its wings on the night, I hurry
so the kids at the church preschool next door
won't ask what I'm doing.

My shovel reveals red roots
buried wires, live   I think,   *arteries*
in the damp dirt that is so much more accommodating
than the dust of the west.

I think of Bannack, Montana,
when we sat in antique schoolroom desks,
peered out the narrow windows of the Hotel Meade,
and my sister asked   *If this is a ghost town, where are the graves?*

This morning I woke at 4:00,
the kitten I found yesterday by my shoulder.
She had soiled herself
and when I lifted her head, there was only weight.
I transferred her body to a towel,
and washed her,
as one might with a wedding ring.

Now, I bring her outside in a plastic Walmart bag
but can't bear the way it looks in the ground
                    like trash
so I unwrap it
and when I pick her up, the body curls gently
into a gray circle, a cat moon, a lone satellite
in the earth.

An order replays in the echoing caves
of my ear or brain:
Take off your shoes, for you stand on holy ground.

Across the street, the ambulances test their sirens in short whoops.
On my knee: a red ant. Winged.
Some insects move so quickly   but without grace.

From the window, my tomcat watches,
his eyes golden,
                    jewel-bright moons.
I wonder if he knows what I'm doing,
what has happened,
what must, someday, happen to him.

PROCESSIONAL

We crossed the bridge into Kentucky
the day after summer solstice,
hills dark green in the fading light and warm rain,
sprinkled crystal confetti, on the windshield.

To our left, the oil refinery rose up
like a mini Oz, a magic city,
lights climbing over all the stacks and steeples.
Almost beautiful—if you didn't know what it was.

It could be a church spanning acres
if it wasn't for the spouts of flame
shooting obscenely from tall chimneys,
bearing their torches against the Appalachian night.

We think of this country as young
though its land is the same age as the earth itself.
Yet it *feels* younger—not having hosted enough people
to completely dull the complexion of the land.

We know we're home when we drive over the Monongahela,
swollen with storm drainage, bright brown,
the artery that sustains the region.
Despite living here for years, I haven't touched its waters.

RELIEF EFFORTS

A dead monarch rests like a leaf against the sidewalk,
its stained-glass panels punched out—half a wing short,
while the air burns pleasantly toward September.
Meanwhile, my skin sutures itself more quickly than expected.

For the second time today, I watch two dragonflies
clasped together in the shimmering heat,
fly as one insect. Each season I grow
a little more jealous, a little less sure.

NIGHT GARDEN

If only the little constellation maps were what the night sky really looked like, complete with connecting lines. Though we'd like to think differently, the truth is that there are no swans, queens, harps, or warriors—just silver decay a long way off. Tonight, the grapes have dropped, too sour to eat, and orb weavers have strung their banners. I plucked the katydid from a stray strand and let it go. Though that pleasant September smoke is back, my autumnal sister carries a new emptiness, so I do, too. This summer, I let the weeds have their way with the east flower bed. *Take care*, someone says. I wish I knew how.

LOVE POEM

Soap splashes the windshield
in a ribbons of pink, yellow, and blue.

This chrysalis of glass and steel seals us in a sanctum,
the cloth flagella envelop us on all sides,

and I am grateful for the distraction
of this gentle magic carpet ride.

Outside, the September sun goes stale in a cornflower sky;
I grow sluggish as flies on a windowsill, their buzzing syrupy,

a slow dance. I lean too heavily on you, I know—
taking without giving, requiring so much assurance.

Water comets streak past us as my heart takes up residence in my throat.
Artificial scent—green apple—intrudes through the vents.

Later, in the dark, we will lie back to back; you asleep
me looking out on the spectral night, its fog-shawled stillness.

I don't deserve this love, but will take it anyway,
greedily, each day of my life.

SOMNAMBULANCE

Out the kitchen window
the night is in zenith,
and the lone, soap-yellow streetlight
hangs filmy luminescence
on summer mist,
spectral in its stillness.

> I have no reason to hurt.
> Still, jealousy splits me open.
> They say the shivering your heart feels
> in these situations
> is just a release of cortisol.
> *Just.*

Drawn to the little brown book
of my great grandmother's poems,
I read about a life stained with tea,
embroidered with roses. Winter was her season.
For her, the branches were fairy dusted,
the frigid air: mother-of-pearl.

> She had faith in the landscape.
> God, too. Willing to forgive
> the rough edges in both.
> The streetlight blinks. Once, twice.
> I empty my glass in the sink,
> return, uneasily, to sleep.

FIELD NOTES

This morning the grass was glazed
and the mushrooms had lost their yellow blush.

Another blue jay thumped against the dining room window.

I wondered:
> how many birds lay dying in the world?
> how many nests are pulled apart by children's fingers?
> at what point does an egg, swallowed whole, collapse?

I googled these questions
and for the rest of the day felt like a dried flower in an old book.

Maybe later I'll tell my sister
how the hills here look like theatre props—
painted cardboard that rolls in during a scene change.

Some nights   dimly,
you can hear the stadium   singing
misty taste of moonshine
teardrops in my eye

What I'd like to see   is a fox cross a road
and make it to the other side with all its softness still on its body.

I make a list of things to ignore:

> the river in its dirty green dress,
> the coal trucks steaming down Beechurst,
> the anxiety simmering gently in my chest.

8 HOT NEW TIPS

1. The honeysuckle will bloom limp, yellow hands.
Hold the flower and pinch / just above the calyx.
Pinch hard enough to break through the petal
but not all the way to the insides.
>   You'll see what I mean.

2. Mix things up by imagining someone else
spraying poison up the chimney, knocking egg sacs down.

3. Try keeping your clothes on / as you walk into the river.
It will be uncomfortable going in / and again, coming out.

4. The dryer will sing in the basement. Don't be afraid
to roll the lint into a ball / the color of a storm.

5. Leave the lights on.
I mean all of them.
I mean the bulb in the refrigerator.
I mean Ursa Minor
and the oxidized sconce on the corner of the garage
scratched / and full of bugs.

6. Brush your teeth. Stare at the enamel / basin.
Wonder if the dead russet rat, soggy and fat, was a dream.

7. Use your hands / bare / to collect worms
when they drown up from the ground.

8. Collect also / the first branch that brushes against your hat.
Put it in your bag like it's something worth saving.
Better yet, plant it in the ground. See what it has to give.

THE INCALCULABLE LOSS OF A SMALL THING

The ring left on the edge of a motel sink,
a dress gone from its hanger,
sweet pea shuttering its blooms at summer's end—
absence insists on announcing itself.

Forgiveness: another way to purge.
I prayed   *Just this once*—

When I call my dad, I hear his replies
mostly as echoes of another voice.
Sometimes, measuring distance in miles makes things easier.

He never mentions what he must see daily:
the wiry threads of pigment in an iris,
blood vessels branching in silhouette,
milky ghosts blooming in the lens.

If I had the courage, I would tell him
there is no reason to shoot a coyote
for being a coyote.

I would tell him there is no tunnel of my heart
that hasn't been picked clean.

In "A Place to Lie Down," the italicized line is quoted from the *National Geographic* article, "Do Bugs Sleep? Why They're Surprisingly Similar to People" by Liz Langley, published 16 May 2015.

Lines in "Wild Tonic in the Rain" were influenced by Mary Ann Samyn's poem, "An Ideal Situation" (*Air, Light, Dust, Shadow, Distance*, 42 Miles Press).

"Attic of the Skull" takes its title from a line in Sylvia Plath's poem, "Two Lovers and a Beachcomber by the Real Sea."

The last line in "Am I the Only One Here" is influenced by the last line in Susan Goslee's poem, "After Kawabata's *Thicket*."

The first line in "Glue Market" is from *The Great Gatsby* and the form is modeled after Kelly Ricken's untitled poem in Idaho State University's *Black Rock & Sage,* Issue 13 (2014).

The mountain in "Equity" and "Summit" is Sawtell(e) Peak in the Caribou-Targhee National Forest.

The last line of "Fourth of July" was inspired by a line in Beth Bachmann's poem "Elegy" (*Temper*, University of Pittsburgh Press).

"Field Notes" quotes lyrics from John Denver's song, "Take Me Home, Country Roads."

Grateful acknowledgement is made to the editors of the following journals, in which these poems first appeared, sometimes in different forms:

Appalachian Review: "Suburban Orchestral"
Arcturus Magazine: "Every Seven Years" and "Morning Glory Pool"
Atlas and Alice: "8 Hot New Tips"
Atticus Review: "In My Desert"
Barnstorm: "Return to Sender"
Berkeley Poetry Review: "Wild Tonic in the Rain"
Blue Earth Review: "Horoscope"
The Boiler: "Interior Architecture"
The Carolina Quarterly: "Dormancies" and "Fear of Loss at Any Moment"
The Cincinnati Review: "Coralbone Bloom"
The Citron Review: "Am I the Only One Here"
Coal Hill Review: "Pleasant Ghosts"
Columbia Journal: "What You're Really Looking For"
Cosmonauts Avenue: "I Hear You're Doing a Great Job"
Dogwood: A Journal of Poetry and Prose: "A Hiding Place, a Surprise"
The Emerson Review: "Attic of the Skull"
The Evansville Review: "Love Poem"
Fifth Wednesday Journal Plus: "Liquor Outlet"
Flyway: Journal of Writing & Environment: "The Incalculable Loss of a Small Thing," "Topography Pacific," "Another Small Failure"
Glassworks: "Sunflowers in the Median"
Hawai'i Pacific Review: "Dear Astoria"
The Hopper: "Under the Broom Tree"
The Journal: "My Mother Sent Cards"
JuxtaProse: "Immersion"
The Lascaux Review: "Summit"
The Laurel Review: "Genealogy," "Gravedigging, 5:00 AM," "Overlook"
Meridian: "Diorama of Anxiety Attack"
the minnesota review: "A Place to Lie Down"
The Penn Review: "Good Vibrations"
The Pinch: "Divination" and "Punchline"
Poet Lore: "Torpor"
Radar Poetry: "Interview"
Ruminate: "Dust on Horses" and "Glue Market"
Silk Road Review: "Fourth of July"

Sou'wester: "Search Party (I.)" and "Search Party (II.)"
Spoon River Poetry Review: "Dear Idaho—"
Tinderbox Poetry Journal: "The Bravery of Cotton"

Some of these poems also appeared in the chapbook *Attic of the Skull* (dancing girl press, 2018).

I am grateful to West Virginia University's MFA program, and to the English Department at Idaho State University. These poems would not have been possible without dedicated teachers at every level, and my special thanks goes to Mary Ann Samyn and Susan Goslee; I can never repay you for the guidance you've given.

I am eternally grateful to Autumn House Press and Mike Good in particular for expertly shepherding this collection into the world.

Thank you to my peers and fellow writers, especially Bryce Berkowitz, Kelsey Englert, Elizabeth Leo, Maggie Montague, Sarah Munroe, Mike Nichols, Kuniko Poole, Jordan Radford, Shannon Sankey, the students in WVU's MFA program, and everyone who has given me feedback or writing advice.

For everyone who encouraged me along the way—each compliment, each "like" on Facebook, each email exchange, each instance of taking time out of your day to read my poems—thank you.

And to Bridget and Tim, for being my shade in the desert.

Natalie Homer's poetry has been published in *The Cincinnati Review, The Boiler, Berkeley Poetry Review, Meridian, Barnstorm, The Carolina Quarterly, The Pinch*, and elsewhere. She received an MFA from West Virginia University and works as a parish administrator of an Episcopal Church. Originally from Idaho, she now lives in Waynesburg, Pennsylvania with her husband and cats.

New and Forthcoming Releases

American Home by Sean Cho A.
Winner of the 2020 Autumn House Chapbook Prize
selected by Danusha Laméris

Under the Broom Tree by Natalie Homer

Molly by Kevin Honold
Winner of the 2020 Autumn House Fiction Prize
selected by Dan Chaon

The Animal Indoors by Carly Inghram
Winner of the 2020 CAAPP Book Prize
selected by Terrance Hayes

speculation, n. by Shayla Lawz
Winner of the 2020 Autumn House Poetry Prize
selected by Ilya Kaminsky

All Who Belong May Enter by Nicholas Ward
Winner of the 2020 Autumn House Nonfiction Prize
selected by Jaquira Díaz

The Gardens of Our Childhoods by John Belk
Winner of the 2021 Rising Writer Prize in Poetry
selected by Matthew Dickman

Myth of Pterygium by Diego Gerard Morrison
Winner of the 2021 Rising Writer Prize in Fiction
selected by Maryse Meijer

Out of Order by Alexis Sears
Winner of the 2021 Donald Justice Poetry Prize
selected by Quincy Lehr

Queer Nature: A Poetry Anthology edited by Michael Walsh

AUTUMN HOUSE PRESS

For our full catalog please visit: http://www.autumnhouse.org